IMAGES OF WAR

HITLER'S PANTHER TANK BATTALIONS 1943–45

RARE PHOTOGRAPHS FROM WARTIME ARCHIVES

Ian Baxter

Pen & Sword
MILITARY

First published in Great Britain in 2020 by
PEN & SWORD MILITARY
An imprint of
Pen & Sword Books Ltd
47 Church Street
Barnsley
South Yorkshire
S70 2AS

ISBN 978-1-52676-545-1

A CIP catalogue record for this book is available from the British Library.

Typeset by Concept, Huddersfield, West Yorkshire HD4 5JL
Printed and bound in England by CPI Group (UK) Ltd, Croydon CR0 4YY

FSC www.fsc.org MIX Paper from responsible sources FSC® C013604

Pen & Sword Books Limited incorporates the imprints of Atlas, Archaeology, Aviation, Discovery, Family History, Fiction, History, Maritime, Military, Military Classics, Politics, Select, Transport, True Crime, Air World, Frontline Publishing, Leo Cooper, Remember When, Seaforth Publishing, The Praetorian Press, Wharncliffe Local History, Wharncliffe Transport, Wharncliffe True Crime and White Owl.

For a complete list of Pen & Sword titles please contact
PEN & SWORD BOOKS LIMITED
47 Church Street, Barnsley, South Yorkshire S70 2AS, England
E-mail: enquiries@pen-and-sword.co.uk
Website: www.pen-and-sword.co.uk

Contents

About the Author

Ian Baxter is a military historian who specialises in German twentieth-century military history. He has written more than fifty books including *Poland – The Eighteen Day Victory March, Panzers In North Africa, The Ardennes Offensive, The Western Campaign, The 12th SS Panzer-Division Hitlerjugend, The Waffen-SS on the Western Front, The Waffen-SS on the Eastern Front, The Red Army at Stalingrad, Elite German Forces of World War II, Armoured Warfare, German Tanks of War, Blitzkrieg, Panzer-Divisions at War, Hitler's Panzers, German Armoured Vehicles of World War Two, Last Two Years of the Waffen-SS at War, German Soldier Uniforms and Insignia, German Guns of the Third Reich, Defeat to Retreat: The Last Years of the German Army At War 1943–45, Operation Bagration – the Destruction of Army Group Centre, German Guns of the Third Reich, Rommel and the Afrika Korps, U-Boat War*, and most recently *The Sixth Army and the Road to Stalingrad*. He has written over a hundred articles including 'Last days of Hitler', 'Wolf's Lair', 'The Story of the V1 and V2 Rocket Programme', 'Secret Aircraft of World War Two', 'Rommel at Tobruk', 'Hitler's War With his Generals', 'Secret British Plans to Assassinate Hitler', 'The SS at Arnhem', 'Hitlerjugend', 'Battle of Caen 1944', 'Gebirgsjäger at War', 'Panzer Crews', 'Hitlerjugend Guerrillas', 'Last Battles in the East', 'The Battle of Berlin', and many more. He has also reviewed numerous military studies for publication, supplied thousands of photographs and important documents to various publishers and film production companies worldwide, and lectures to various schools, colleges and universities throughout the United Kingdom and the Republic of Ireland.

Introduction

In 1943 the Panzerwaffe provided the backbone of Germany's offensive and defensive measures on the battlefield. The Germans were well aware that they needed powerful tanks to counter Soviet T-34 medium and KV-1 heavy tanks, which were superior to anything the Panzerwaffe had available at the time. Henschel had produced the Tiger I, the largest tank in the Panzerwaffe, well gunned and armoured. The steel of its frontal hull and turret armour was 100mm thick, the turret gun mantlet 120mm, the hull side-plates 60mm, the side superstructure 80mm, and the turret sides 80mm. It mounted a long 8.8cm KwK 36 gun and its main purpose on the battlefield was for offensive breakthroughs. However, by the time it became operational, the military situations on both the Eastern Front and in North Africa had changed considerably. Instead of offensive actions its main use was now considered defensive, being used primarily as a mobile anti-tank and infantry gun support weapon.

To sustain the Tiger on the battlefield and help defeat the increasingly strong enemy armour, German tacticians knew that the Tiger required more and heavier tank support. Already in 1942 designers had been putting together a new tank weighing 30 tonnes to support the Tiger. It was named the Panther and was classed as a medium tank. It had an ordnance inventory designation of Sd.Kfz.171. The Panther was intended not only to counter heavy Soviet tanks, but also to replace the Pz.Kpfw.III and Pz.Kpfw.IV (the Panzer III and the Panzer IV). The Panther would serve alongside the Pz.Kpfw.IV and the heavier Tiger I for the rest of the war.

The Panther was much cheaper to manufacture than the Tiger I, and only slightly more expensive than the Pz.Kpfw.IV. The tank's design too, such as its armour, final drive and transmission, was simplified to improve production rates and combat raw material shortages.

In January 1943 the first Panthers, known as Ausführung D, left the production line, after which various modifications were undertaken to improve the vehicle including the engine and its armour plating. The tank was armed with the Rheinmetall-Borsig 7.5cm KwK42 (L/70) with semi-automatic shell ejection. For local defence the tank had two MG34 guns featuring an armoured barrel sleeve. An MG34 was located coaxially with the main gun on the gun mantlet with an identical MG34 on the glacis plate. This was fired by the radio operator.

The tank had a five-man crew comprising the commander, gunner, loader, driver and radio operator. The commander, loader and gunner were in the turret, while the driver and radio operator were in the hull. The driver always sat on the front left side of the tank, and next to him was the machine gunner whose job it was to operate the radio.

For operations the Panther formed Panzer Abteilung 51 (Tank Battalion 51) on 9 January, and then Panzer Abteilung 52 on 6 February 1943. These battalions would be deployed to critical sectors, either for breakthrough operations or, more typically, counter-attacks. Supporting the Panther, apart from the Pz.Kpfw.IV, was a host of other vehicles: the Sd.Kfz.7/1, Sd.Kfz.9, Sd.Kfz.10, Sd.Kz.251 halftrack, the Bergepanther armoured recovery vehicle, and smaller vehicles such as the Sd.Kfz.2 Kettenkrad, motorcycles and motorcycle combinations, Kübelwagen, and support truck elements comprising infantry, panzergrenadiers, and maintenance teams.

The battalion was organised into a staff company comprising a communications platoon of various armoured reconnaissance and communication vehicles, and engineer and anti-aircraft platoons. The panzer company, which consisted of three platoons, four tanks in each, was accompanied by medical service and repair vehicles. There was also a workshop company consisting of two workshop platoons with a recovery platoon, communications, armourer, and a spare part detachment. This was what was required to maintain the Panther in fighting condition.

Due to the severe situations of 1943, the Panther was rushed to the front before all of its mechanical problems had been corrected. Reliability was considerably improved over time, but some of the design flaws, such as its weak final drive units, were never corrected. The Panther was to make its debut on the Eastern Front in the largest tank battle of the war.

(**Opposite, above**) As the war progressed there was a great need for more heavy tanks that would be able to deal with the growing strength of Russian armour. Through 1942 designers began putting together the Pz.Kpfw.V prototype, known as the Panther. In this photograph a turretless Panther is being put through a series of factory trials to see if the tank is watertight.

(**Opposite, below**) At the factory the underbelly of the Panther hull is being inspected. The chassis of the Panther mounted eight sets of interleaved road wheels or bogies on either side. The road wheels were carried on twin torsion bars lying transversely across the vehicle.

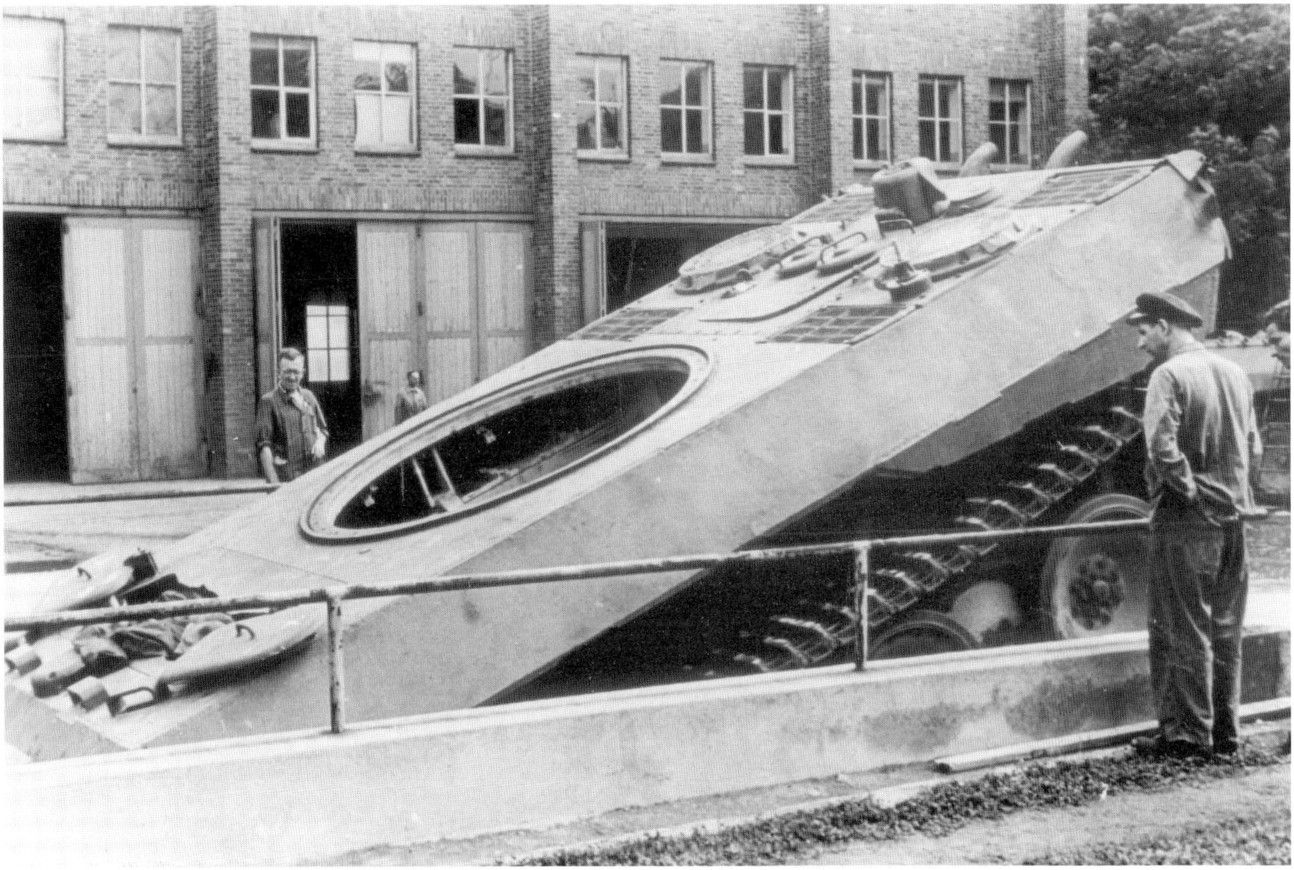

Standing in a water tank, factory specialists check to see whether water has leaked into the Panther engine compartment. This test was for amphibious wading and to see if the engine compartment seals leaked. The engine was housed in the rear of the hull and was flanked on each side by two radiators and extracting fans. Although the powerful Maybach engine fared well under various tests, it was extremely complicated. Despite the tests, when the Panther first fought on the battlefield some of the vehicles overheated and leaked water.

Being put through a series of trials to get this Panther Ausf.D battle-ready. This photograph was taken in early 1943 on the proving grounds of Grafenwöhr. The vehicle still retains the Panther number '163' painted in white large numbers on the turret side. The crew are trialling the vehicle wading through water, which soon proved its undoing at Kursk when water leaked into the engine compartments of many of the Panthers.

The same Panther, 163, being put through its paces during trials in early 1943. Despite mechanical problems the Panther had an impressive main armament that was also a superb accurate anti-tank gun. In tests it could hit a target 2.0m × 2.5m wide 100 per cent of the time at 1,500m using the Pzgr 39/42 round. These levels of accuracy could not be achieved under battlefield conditions, but gunners would soon learn to be very accurate.

(**Opposite, above**) The crew of this Panther Ausf.D pose for the camera before its trails in early 1943. Hitler insisted that the Panther be ready for what became the largest tank battle in military history around Kursk. In fact the Führer was so instant on the Panther being ready he delayed the attack to give manufacturers time to sort out teething problems.

(**Above**) An interesting photograph showing a column of Panthers halted on a muddy road during a training exercise in early 1943. The leading Panther has the factory number '116' painted in white on the turret side.

(**Opposite, below**) This Panther Ausf.D crew rest during a pause in a training exercise before the tanks' release to the front. Note the track links attached to the side of the vehicle for added protection. The tank also carries candle smoke dischargers bolted onto the turret sides. Although not very clear, the tank still has the factory number '133' painted on the turret.

(**Opposite, above**) A crew member poses for the camera next to a Panther Ausf.D. This photograph shows a nice view of the 7.5cm KwK 42 L/70 rifled cannon with canvas sheeting protecting the muzzle brake from dust and dirt. The purpose of the muzzle brake was to shorten the recoil. With the amount of smoke and gas that the barrel produced on firing, a barrel fumes extractor was introduced in April 1943 to prevent gases entering the fighting compartment.

(**Opposite, below**) The crew of a Panther Ausf.D pose for the camera with their tank during a training exercise. The vehicle still carries its factory colour of a yellow sand base application, which would be painted over when it was moved to the front. Many of the Panthers that saw action during the summer of 1943 had a standard colour of dark yellow with light random mottle patterns of olive green and red brown. Note the candle smoke dischargers on the turret side. These were discontinued in June 1943, though some Panthers continued to carry them for a few months until they were finally removed.

(**Above**) Three Panthers can be seen on a training exercise. The middle Panther's large factory numbers can still be seen painted in white on the turret sides.

Chapter One

Eastern Front Battles (1943)

Through the first half of 1943 German Army Group Centre had maintained the strategic initiative on the Eastern Front, so Hitler decided to undertake a massive offensive that he was convinced would bring him victory. Kursk, he believed, would be the key. The attack would be launched against a huge salient 120 miles wide and 75 miles deep, the greatest tank battle ever. It would include the bulk of his mighty Panzerwaffe, among them his elite Waffen-SS divisions.

In June 1943 plans for the battle at Kursk were issued to all the commanders in the field. The codename for the attack was Citadel or *Zitadelle*. The German force was to be distributed between the northern and southern groups, consisting of twenty-two divisions in total, six of which were Panzer and five Panzergrenadier. The main attack fell to 9th Army in the north, where there were to be 335,000 soldiers, 590 tanks and 424 assault guns. But in the south the Germans fielded an even stronger force: 350,000 troops, 1,269 tanks and 245 assault guns. Just putting together such a strong force was a great achievement. Many troops had been lost the previous winter.

The new Panther tanks of Abteilung 51 had been transported from Grafenwöhr to the area of Army Group South at Kharkov in late June. They formed up with Panzer Abteilung 52 of Pz.Rgt.Stb 39.

During this period Panzer Abteilungen 51 and 52 received ninety-six Panther Ausf.Ds in each battalion, and also two Panthers without turrets which were modified as recovery vehicles, known as the Berge-Schlepper.

On 1 July Panzer Abteilung 51 arrived in the area of Tomarovka and prepared its positions to attack, while Panzer Abteilung 52 drove towards Novo Borrisowka. Both Panzer battalions were subordinated to the staff of Panzer Regiment 39 and formed 'Panther Lauchert', named after the commander Major Meinrad von Lauchert. Panther Lauchert was then attached to Panzer Grenadier Division Großdeutschland, which in turn was part of the 4th Panzer Army in Army Group South.

Even as Panther Lauchert prepared its force for action, a number of vehicles developed problems. Some Panthers overheated, and six caught fire from leaking fuel. As Lauchert's Panthers arrived in their final assembly areas, 174 were combat-ready.

When the time came to attack, Lauchert's Panthers advanced south-east of Butovo through a series of minefields and heavily-defended Soviet positions. By the afternoon of the first day, Panzer Abteilung 51 reported only twenty-two Panther tanks in service. Twenty-eight were destroyed, the remainder damaged. The remaining Panthers, supported by well-armed grenadiers, continued through the Russian defences, but the Germans had underestimated their strength and depth.

By the evening of 10 July it was reported that only ten operational Panthers were left in the front line. It was estimated that 60 per cent could be easily repaired; forty already had been and were on their way back to the front. Both sides had suffered heavy losses, but while for the Russians there were always more men and machines where they had come from, this was not so for the Germans. Within a week of Zitadelle, both sides had lost several hundred tanks and thousands of troops. While the Red Army and the Germans were both able to repair their broken tanks, only the Russians were able to replace them. The Panzerwaffe had to struggle on with what they had left.

The Russians had committed seven corps to the battle with more than 850 tanks and SU-85 assault guns. When the Soviet tanks ran out of ammunition, the crews often physically rammed the German tanks. Dismounted tanks crews then set about destroying the Panzers on foot using any weapon at their disposal, including grenades and mines.

In the Battle of Kursk the Panther demonstrated its capacity to destroy any Soviet armoured fighting vehicle from long distance and had a high kill rate. However, its success was severely hampered by its mechanical problems and the strong Russian defensive lines.

By 15 July the Germans had irretrievably lost the battle of Kursk, and the German forces in the south bore the brunt of the consequent Soviet drive. The Russian Voronezh and Steppe fronts possessed massive local superiority against everything the Germans had on the battlefield, including tanks and assault guns. The Panzerwaffe now had to improvise with what they had.

After Kursk the number of Panthers were slowly built up again, and it was hoped that it in future they could be made more reliable. Also, by August 1943 an improved Panther variant was already in production. The Ausführung A included a number of detail alterations to the turret and increased armour thickness in some areas of the chassis. Some late Ausf.D variants and all Ausf.A models were equipped with an improved Maybach engine, increasing power from 650 to 700 horsepower.

In August 1943 the Waffen-SS Panzer divisions Leibstandarte, Totenkopf and Wiking all received a single company of the new modified Panther Ausf.D. The 1st Battalion, SS Panzer Regiment Das Reich, also received forty-nine improved Ausf.D Panthers to equip two of its tank companies plus its regimental staff company. In late August the battalion re-joined the Das Reich Division at the front and began operating successfully. But by the end of 1943 Das Reich had lost all forty-nine of its Panthers, the last in fighting around Zhitomir in the Ukraine.

One of the main reasons for these high losses was that the tanks were rarely permanently assigned to a single division or corps but shuffled around according to the situation on the battlefield. This type of warfare was demanding for the Panthers. During the winter of 1943 there were on average 2,000 tanks in all the Panzer units on the Eastern Front, of which 800 were combat-ready at any one time. It was indeed a small force for such a large front to cover. Panther units were compelled to try to fill the gaps in the infantry and hold the front. Through November and December 1943 the Panther force fought well and had some success.

During the autumn of 1943, when many Ausf.As began to enter service, Hitler decided to give an entire battalion of Panthers to each Waffen-SS Panzer Division to replace their existing under-gunned and under-armoured mid-range Pz.Kpfw.III. Hitler was determined that the fortunes of the Eastern Front would be decided using the Panther and Tiger as the backbone to the victory that would soon be his.

A Panther Ausf.D awaiting to be shipped to the front in April or May 1943. These tanks were shipped on special flat cars that could be quickly loaded and unloaded. For the remainder of the war, this type of transportation would be the best way to move armour from one part of the front to another. Note the long column of Panthers being readied for shipment.

(**Above**) An Ausf.D which has just been loaded onto a flatcar and chocked for its journey to the front. There was a great expectation for the Panther at Kursk in July 1943, however there were too few to make any real impact during the battle.

(**Opposite, above**) A Panther rolls along a road bound for the front. For the Kursk offensive the Panthers were brought to the front for action. They were distributed into two new Panther battalions: the 51st and 52nd. These arrived on 30 June and 1 July and were attached to the Großdeutschland Division in the XLVIII Panzer Corps of Army Group South. This Panzer Corps was commanded by General Otto von Knobelsdorff and consisted of the 3rd and 11th Panzer Divisions and the 167th Infantry Division.

(**Opposite, below**) A Panther during a fire mission. The Panther first made its debut on the Eastern Front at Kursk in July 1943. It was rushed into battle before it was fully ready for combat. Its main armament was the 7.5cm KwK 42 (L/70) with semi-automatic shell ejection. It was regarded at Kursk as one of the most powerful tanks on the battlefield due to its large propellant charge and the long barrel, which gave it a very high muzzle velocity and armour-piercing capability.

Three Panthers have halted in a field and Soviet PoWs can be seen resting before being sent to the rear.

A Panther during the Kursk offensive. In the distance armour can be seen spread out across the steppe during the initial stages of the campaign. In June 1943 there were twenty-one Panzer divisions, including four Waffen-SS divisions and two Panzergrenadier divisions, being prepared for Operation Zitadelle in the Kursk salient.

A Panther tank belonging to the 51st Abteilung advancing across a field to the Kursk offensive. The 51st Abteilung consisted of ninety-six Panthers at Kursk. The Abteilung attacked in waves, with the unit echeloned in depth, one battalion after the other.

Two tank men converse next to a stationary Panther during the Kursk offensive. For the attack the Panzerwaffe were determined to rejuvenate their Blitzkrieg tactics, but the immense preparations that had gone into constructing the Soviet defences meant that the Panzerwaffe were never going to succeed penetrating the Red Army fortifications.

On a steppe during the Kursk campaign are a number of Panther tanks belonging to the 51st Abteilung. For the offensive this battalion and the 52nd came under the control of Major von Lauchert's improvised brigade staff, which was equipped with eight Panthers. It fought alongside the Panzergrenadier Division Grossdeutschland as part of the southern prong of the attack.

Two Panther Ausf.Ds halted during a pause in operations at Kursk. These tanks belong to the 8th Kompanie Panzer Abteilung 52. During the battle the battalion experienced numerous mechanical issues with the Panther, including: engine overheating, fuel leaks, and failures in the transmission and the final drives.

On the Eastern Front and a tank man poses for the camera in front of his Panther in the summer of 1943. The vehicle is being repaired and one of its road wheels has been removed. The Panther could operate with missing or broken wheels, but the interleaved wheel system meant replacing inner wheels was time-consuming. The interleaved wheels had a tendency to become clogged with mud, rocks and ice, and could freeze solid overnight.

(**Opposite**) Two photographs taken in sequence showing Panthers undergoing trials in the summer of 1943. In spite of the initial mechanical problems the Panther became an excellent battle tank. It combined a fearsome blend of firepower, armour and mobility, outclassing the Soviet T-34. However, by the time these vehicles entered service they were up against a much more formidable foe than the Germans had encountered when they first invaded Russia in 1941.

(**Above**) A crewman of a Panther Ausf.D poses for the camera in front of his tank. The vehicle belongs to the 4th Panzer Regiment. On the Eastern Front the Panthers were arranged into tactical formations known as 'Panzerkeil'. This was an armoured wedge spearheaded by heavy tanks to punch forward through Russian anti-tank defences. The Panthers would often advance alongside Tigers with the Pz.Kpfw.IIIs and IVs protecting their flanks.

(**Above**) A Panther Ausf.D appears to have been put out of action and the crew are removing the tank's ammunition. All the ammunition for the main armament was stored in the hull with eighteen rounds stored next to the turret on each side. The main gun for this variant used two different types of ammunition: APCB-HE (Panzergranate 39/42) and HE (Sprenggranate 42) shells.

(**Opposite, above**) On the advance are Panther Ausf Ds of Panzer Grenadier Division Großdeutschland during operations in August 1943. After the Kursk offensive was cancelled, the division was transferred back to Army Group Centre and resumed its role as a mobile reserve. Both Panthers and Tigers were expanded to a battalion. The battalion of the Panzer Regiment Großdeutschland saw heavy fighting around Karachev before being transferred back to XLVIII Panzer Corps in late August.

(**Opposite, below**) Two Panthers have halted in a field. Both appear to have seen heavy combat, indicated by missing and damaged side skirts (*Schürzen*). One crewman is evidently trying to remove one section of Schürzen from the tank. The vehicle consisted of six Schürzen plates either side.

Achtung!
Ladung zu breit!

(**Opposite, above**) A Panther Ausf.A chocked and ready to be transported to the front on a flatbed rail car. The tank still retains its factory sand base colour. This second production series model was built by MAN, Daimler-Benz, Demag and MNH and 2,000 of them entered service between August 1943 and May 1944. The design of the Ausf.A incorporated a ball-mounted hull machine gun, a further modified gear box and transmission, strengthened road wheels and additional coolant tubes to reduce the risk of engine fires.

(**Opposite, below**) Two Panther Ausf.Ds and a Pz.Kpfw.IV Ausf.E somewhere in Russia in the summer of 1943. Both Panthers have had a field workshop applied coat of Zimmerit anti-magnetic mine paste applied over the chassis.

(**Above**) An excellent photograph showing the driver of a Panther during operations in 1943. This tank belongs to the SS Wiking Division. In late July and August the SS Panzer Divisions Leibstandarte, Totenkopf and Wiking each received a single company of modified Ausf.D Panthers. In the same period, the 1st Battalion, SS Panzer Regiment Das Reich, also received forty-nine modified Panther Ausf.Ds to equip two of its tank companies.

(**Above**) A Panther from an SS Division Totenkopf Panther battalion rolling along a road on the Eastern Front. A typical SS Panther battalion in theory fielded seventy-six Panthers, four companies each with seventeen tanks and a headquarters company with a further eight Panthers, including three command variants. In addition, the panzer regiment's staff company consisted of a further three command Panthers, bringing the divisional total to seventy-nine Panthers, including six command tanks.

(**Opposite, above**) A Panther Ausf.A belonging to an SS battalion has been knocked out of action in 1943. After Kursk the Waffen-SS would receive an entire battalion of Panthers to replace their existing Pz.Kpfw.III-equipped battalion.

(**Opposite, below**) A Panther man caught by the camera either working or resting on the tube housing the gun barrel cleaning rods. The 'drum' cupola and skirt armour identifies this tank as a Panther Ausf.D2 on the Eastern Front during operations in 1943. The tank is complete with smoke candle dischargers.

245

A crewman dressed in his familiar black panzer uniform poses for the camera with a partially concealed Panther Ausf.D. Tarpaulin has been draped over the front glacis of the tank indicating that the vehicle is undergoing some maintenance or having its machine gun changed or overhauled.

The crew of an Sd.Kfz.231 (8-rad) converse with crew members from another vehicle during a pause in their mission.

During a reconnaissance mission and an Sd.Kfz.222 and 223 can be seen stationary in a field whilst a returning unit of Volkswagen Schwimmwagens arrive with the crew raising their right arm, probably hailing a successful operation.

Chapter Two

Italian Warfare (1943–44)

While the Germans tried to contain the Soviet forces from pushing westwards on the Eastern Front, in the southern theatre, in Italy, the Wehrmacht were now compelled to try to restrain an Allied invasion of Sicily which started in July 1943. The invasion was a combined Allied amphibious attack along the shores of Sicily at the Gulf of Gela comprising the US Seventh Army and the British Eighth Army.

The resisting German and Italian forces were unable to prevent the Allied capture of the island, but they did succeed in evacuating the bulk of their of their troops to the mainland, with the last leaving on 17 August 1943. What followed after the capture of Sicily was the mainland Allied invasion of Italy in early September 1943. The German forces, under the command of Field Marshal Albert Kesselring, were ordered to prepare a series of temporary defensive lines across Italy, south of Rome, to buy time to prepare the two permanent defensive lines, the Winter and Gustav Lines, west of the Apennine Mountains. Panther and Tiger tanks were used for this.

The Panther was regarded as particularly formidable in defence. Its turret consisted of the standard Panther turret and its 7.5cm main gun, which was sometimes up-gunned with the 8.8cm mounted on the top of a rectangular box or imbedded in concrete and dug into the ground. The box consisted of two parts, the upper section incorporating the turret ball race and a manhole over an iron ladder down to a second part. This second part was the sleeping compartment for the gun crew and had an escape hatch. These features were to prove their worth along these lines.

Elsewhere on the Italian Front the Panther played a limited role. The terrain was often hilly or mountainous, very different from the open steppes of the Eastern Front. On the whole the Italian campaign was not regarded as one that favoured extensive tank action. However, the Panther still proved its worth. It was found notably in the 16th and 26th Panzer Divisions, forming part of the famous Panzer Regiment 4. The 1st SS Panzer Division 'Leibstandarte' Adolf Hitler (LSSAH), which operated in Italy but did not see combat against the Allies, also received Panther battalions. The SS Panthers were given various duties including guarding major road and rail junctions and undertaking limited anti-partisan operations. It was also involved in operations disarming the Italian army. By the end of 1943, due to the deteriorating situation on the Eastern Front, the LSSAH Division was sent back to Russia.

During 1944 the position in Italy for the Germans had considerably deteriorated. American and British forces were pushing north in spite of sustaining terrible casualties. It took four major offensives between January and May 1944 before the German lines were eventually broken by a combined assault of the Fifth and Eighth Armies. These attacks were concentrated along a twenty-mile front between Monte Cassino and the western seaboard.

To reinforce the defensive lines across Italy there were a number of heavy tank battalions containing both Tigers and Panthers. The heavy Tiger Tank Battalion 508 had been equipped with Panthers and Ferdinand tank destroyers. Often single tanks were moved into combat as parts of the front crumbled.

But armoured defensive action in this area was limited by the terrain and by 4 June Rome fell. The Allies wasted no time and advanced beyond the Italian capital and captured Florence, closing up on the Gothic Line, which was the last major defensive line between Pisa and the Apennines and between Florence and Bologna to the Adriatic coast.

Over the days and weeks to come the Panzerwaffe fought on, defending each position as it fell back. By October 1944, the German lines had been pushed back to northern Italy in the face of overwhelming Allied firepower.

A Panther Ausf.D operating in Italy. The terrain in Italy was not very favourable for tanks and crews found that operations were often limited by mountains and lack of good roads.

A Panther from I Panzer Regiment 4 during occupational operations in Rome during August 1943. Just a month later the Allies landed in Sicily and the German forces, under the command of Field Marshal Albert Kesselring, were ordered to prepare a series of defensive lines across Italy, south of Rome.

A Panther Ausf.A moving along a road in Rome in August 1943. This tank was from I Panzer Regiment 4. These Panthers were given various duties including guarding road and rail junctions and undertaking limited anti-partisan operations. They were also involved in operations disarming the Italian army.

A well camouflaged Panther is being loaded with ammunition during operations in Italy in 1944. In Italy the Panther was found notably in the 16th Panzer Division and the 26th Panzer Division, which formed part of the famous Panzer Regiment 4. The 1st SS Panzer Division 'Leibstandarte' Adolf Hitler (LSSAH) also received Panther battalions in its division, which operated in Italy but did not see combat against the Allies.

A Panther being camouflaged by its crew in 1944 to conceal it from aerial and ground surveillance. At this period of the war in Italy the Allies were causing the Panzerwaffe considerable problems, especially from aerial attacks.

An interesting photograph showing an assortment of armoured vehicles in front of a building in Italy in 1944. From left to right: a Sturmpanzer 'Brummbar', a Panther and two StuG.III Ausf.Gs. The Panzerwaffe relied heavily on assault guns during its defensive operations in Italy.

Parked between two buildings the crew of this Panther Ausf.D are camouflaging the tank during operations near Monte Cassino in the spring of 1944. Fortunately for the Allies these tanks did not operate extensively in Italy.

(**Opposite, above**) Panzergrenadiers can be seen moving along a road with a rear view of a Panther Ausf.A belonging to the 4th Panzer Regiment. This photograph was taken in February 1944. During the early part of that year the Panther Ausf.A fought limited defensive operations. It was not until the spring of 1944 that it became embroiled in heavy fighting against the Allies.

(**Opposite, below**) A Panther belonging to Panzer Regiment 4 advancing along a road during a defensive operation in 1944. Due to the nature of the Italian campaign the Germans were compelled to fight a fixed defensive battle rather than using mobile units.

(**Above**) Two Panthers roll along a road watched by local people.

(**Above**) A Panther rolls through an Italian town bound for the front. Note that vehicle has stowed additional supplies on the turret side to sustain itself on the battlefield for some time.

(**Opposite, above**) A column of late-variant Pz.Kpfw.IVs with intact side-skirts halted on a road inside an Italian town in 1944. These tanks were to be found in Panther battalions supporting the armoured drive.

(**Opposite, below**) A damaged Panther Ausf.A from 1./Pz.Rgt.4 in Italy in 1944. A hit to the rear turret has torn away the rear escape hatch and grab handle. In response to the Allied landings at Anzio–Nettuno in January 1944, the Panzerwaffe dispatched a number of armoured units into the area including the 1./Pz.Rgt.4, which was equipped with seventy-six Panthers.

Chapter Three

Eastern Front (1944)

Through January and February 1944 the military situation for the Germans on the Eastern Front further deteriorated. By the beginning of March, Army Groups A and South still held about half the ground between the Dnieper and the Bug, but in a number of areas the front was buckling under the strain of repeated Soviet attacks. Army Group South was being slowly pressed westwards, its Panzers still unable to strike a decisive counterblow because of the Führer order to stand fast regardless, which meant futile attempts to hold unsuitable positions. By 24 March the Russians had advanced to the Dniester, and a few days later were penetrating the foothills of the Carpathians. Panzerwaffe units that were refused permission by Hitler to withdraw found themselves tied down trying in vain to hold back the Soviet avalanche. These battles became known to the Panzer soldiers as the Kesselschlachten or 'cauldron battles'.

The heavily outnumbered Panthers came to be used as mobile reserves to fight off the more severe attacks, and were also organised into special rescue units to relieve trapped pockets of Germans. One formation specially raised for this purpose was the Heavy Panzer Regiment 'Bäke', named after the much-decorated commander Oberstleutnant Franz Bäke. The regiment consisted of a battalion of Panthers and one of Tigers. It also contained self-propelled artillery, an infantry battalion and engineering units and was so successful on the battlefield that it became the vanguard of the III Panzer Corps.

Elsewhere on the Eastern Front the Panther continued to clock up kills. The improved Ausf.G, which left the factory in February 1944, performed so well that the Waffen-SS were eager to receive these new models. The first elite division to be supplied with large numbers was 5th SS Panzer Division 'Wiking'. By the spring both of the divisions' panzer battalions were re-equipped with a total of 160 Panthers, which was against the policy of allocating just one Panther battalion to each SS armoured division. The 'Wiking' division became the most potent SS armoured formation on the Eastern Front and was used extensively to halt the Soviet drive westwards.

During this period of the war the Panzerwaffe were better supplied with equipment than at any other time on the Eastern Front, thanks to the highly efficient armaments industry. In total some 20,000 fighting vehicles, including 8,328 medium and heavy tanks, 5,751 assault guns, 3,617 tank destroyers and 1,246 self-propelled artillery carriages of various types, reached the Eastern Front. Included in these new arrivals were the second-generation tank-destroyers the Jagdpanzer IV, followed by the Hetzer and then the Jagdpanther and Jagdtiger. The Jagdpanther or 'hunting Panther' boasted a lethal 8.8cm KwK 43 cannon which had been originally fitted on the new Tiger II and mounted on a Panther chassis. This unturreted tank destroyer had thick sloped-armour hull sides, and inside the hull was a roomy interior. For local defence it was armed with an MG34 machine gun fitted in a ball mount on the right side of the front glacis plate. There were two main variants manufactured: the first produced was the 1944 G1 model with a small internally-bolted main-gun mantlet and a modified Panther A engine deck; the later variant, built later in 1944, was known as the G2, which had a larger outside-bolted mantlet and a modified Panther G engine deck. The Jagdpanthers served in the heavy anti-tank battalions, or Schwere Panzerjäger-Abteilung, and operated mainly in Russia. However, they were seen operating in small numbers in July 1944 in Normandy where the 654 Schwere Panzerjäger-Abteilung deployed about a dozen Jagdpanthers against British units. Months later, in the Ardennes offensive in December 1944, larger numbers fought against American units.

The modification of these tanks into tank-destroyers was affirmation of the Panzerwaffe's reluctant duty to undertake a defensive role against overwhelming opposition. They would have to be stretched along a very thin Eastern Front, seldom reaching an effective operating concentration. Panzer divisions too were often broken up and split among hastily constructed battle groups or Kampfgruppe drawn from a motley collection of armoured formations. These battle groups were often put into the line operating well below strength. The demands put upon the Panzerwaffe during the spring and summer of 1944 were onerous: the problems of constant action coupled with the nightmare of not having enough supplies perpetually occupied the minds of the commanders. The Red Army, encouraged by the Germans' dire situation, was now mounting bolder operations against the German front.

One operation unleashed by the Russians was their summer offensive codenamed Operation Bagration. Its objective was to annihilate Army Group Centre. On the morning of 22 June, the third anniversary of the Soviet invasion, Bagration was launched against Army Group Centre. The three German armies opposing them had thirty-seven divisions, weakly supported by armour, against 166 divisions supported by 2,700 tanks and 1,300 assault guns. In front of the Russians the condition of the German forces in Army Group Centre varied considerably. While some parts were demoralised and without sufficient weapons, others were heavily defended with a formidable force. One such powerful formation was the 5th Panzer Division. This was sent directly from the Ukraine by rail to help block the advancing Russian forces on the Moscow-Minsk highway. It was reinforced with 55 Pz.Kpfw.IVs, 70 Panthers, and 29 Tiger Is belonging to the 505th Heavy Tank Battalion.

Other units were also considerably reinforced with Panthers on the German central front, including the 1st Panzer Regiment 'Brandenburg' which was assigned to Panzergrenadier-Division 'Kurmark'. This division contained forty-five Panthers, while Panzer-Regiment 29 of Panzer Division 'Münchenberg' had twenty-one.

In the first week of Bagration the three German armies had lost between them nearly 200,000 men and 900 tanks; 9th Army and the 3rd Panzer Army were almost wiped out. As desperation gripped the battered front lines, troops became heavily reliant on the Tigers and Panthers for defence, but there were never enough available. Again and again these armoured monsters demonstrated their awesome killing power playing a prominent position in Army Group Centre's defence against numerically superior Soviet armoured forces, but with the tide turning against the German army they were overstretched and slowly destroyed. Over the next few days Kurmark and Münchenberg's tank strength was reduced to just twelve Panthers, six Pz.Kpfw.IVs and two or three Tigers.

The remnants of the shattered armies now began trudging back west to rest with what was left of their Panzer units, and refit to build new defensive lines. But any plans to regain the initiative on the Eastern Front were doomed forever.

A Panther being put through trials during the winter of 1944. This vehicle still retains the factory sand colour. When at the front line the crew would apply an application of winter white paint.

322

(**Opposite, above**) A Panther operating on the Eastern Front in early 1944. This tank has an application of white camouflage paint and its body is applied with Zimmerit anti-magnetic mine paste. The paste was applied to all vertical surfaces of the Panther and was designed to prevent the magnetic mines used by Soviet infantry from sticking

(**Opposite, below**) A column of Panthers advance along a snowy road bound for the front. A Panther battalion was often composed of a reconnaissance platoon of five Panthers and a communication platoon of three *Befehls-wagen* Panther Sd.Kfz.267/268. The 1st Company consisted of twenty-two Panthers with each platoon of five Panthers. In total there were four companies to each battalion consisting of twenty-two Panthers.

(**Above**) Whitewashed Panthers advancing across a snow-covered field during operations on the Eastern Front in 1944. By early 1944 the Eastern Front had stabilised following a number of retreats by the Germans.

511

Three photographs taken in sequence showing Panthers on board special flatbed rail cars. The first photo shows the transport of the Panthers arriving at their destination on the Eastern Front and then being unloaded in preparation for operations on the front line. The bulk of German armour was transported by rail; this was the quickest way to move tanks from one place to another.

A stationary Sd.Kfz.232 (8-rad) is seen stationary in a field, partly camouflaged with saplings attached to the vehicle's superstructure. Note the spare wheel attached to its special open roof plate.

A resting Panther crew halt during what appears to be a long march on the Eastern Front during the early winter of 1944. Two fuel drums have been attached to the engine deck.

A Panther appears to be towing a halftrack along a muddy road in the winter of 1944. After a few hours of rain the mud was often enough to immobilize whole columns of wheeled transport, and even tracked vehicles. This was a constant problem throughout the German campaign in Russia.

Waffen-SS Panther's chocked and prepared for distribution to somewhere on the Eastern Front. By 1944 the demands from the frontline from Waffen-SS armoured battalions for Panthers left precious few vehicles available elsewhere for the Panzerwaffe.

The new Panther Ausf.G being prepared to be transported to the front in the spring of 1944. Many of these new tanks were sent to Waffen-SS Panther battalions. The first SS formation to receive them was the 5th SS Panzer Division 'Wiking'. During February 1944 Russian forces almost annihilated the formation in the Korsun Pocket, and its remnants clawed its way back into Poland to be hastily repaired. By the spring both of the division's panzer battalions had been re-equipped with 160 Panthers, making this the most potent Waffen-SS division on the Eastern Front.

Flatbed rail cars carrying what appear to be Panther Ausf.As. Some of the crew are still in the process of securing the tanks to the flatbeds with chains and chocks of wood. These Panthers belong to the 5th SS Panzer Division 'Wiking'. Note that some saplings have been attached to the tanks for camouflage against aerial recognition.

Three photographs showing an independent Panther tank battalion maintenance team undertaking repairs to a Panther. Much was owed to these specialist maintenance companies that kept the tanks in fighting condition. All the photographs show the large portal crane which was used to remove the heavy turret for repairs. After removing the turret, the mechanics were able to place it on special wooden blocks or a wooden horse specially designed for the task. The Panther broke down often, but it could be returned to the battlefield relatively quickly.

FRIES

(**Above**) Two photos in sequence depicting a Panther Ausf.G having its engine removed by an independent Panther tank battalion maintenance crew. A halftrack complete with 6-ton crane hoists the engine into the air. Up to late 1944 the special maintenance companies were able to recover and repair 75 per cent of tanks damaged in combat or broken down due to defect or mechanical problems. Most of the damage to tanks was by anti-tank rifles or mines to the tracks or drive wheels.

(**Opposite**) Two photographs taken in sequence showing a Panther Ausf.G on a road complete with a summer camouflage scheme of dark yellow with oversprayed patches of olive green and red and brown.

Well-armed Panzergrenadiers pass a stationary command Panther during operations on the Eastern Front mid-1944. By this period of the war the German central front was fighting for its life as the Soviets launched Operation Bagration. In a desperate struggle to stem the Russian drive westwards the bulk of the Panther battalions were committed to this operation.

Panzergrenadiers supported by a Panther during a fire mission on the Eastern Front in the summer of 1944. Note the tank tracks bolted to the armoured sides of the Panther for additional armoured protection.

From the turret of a Panther somewhere on the Eastern Front the commander can be seen looking through a pair of binoculars. The tank is approaching a halted Panther. The crew appear to be preparing their vehicle for operations.

A column of Sd.Kfz.250/10s advance along a road supporting the main drive. The Sd.Kfz.250 was designed to provide armoured reconnaissance troops to the Panzer and Panzergrenadier divisions. Later variants often carried 2cm, 3.7cm and even 7.5cm cannons to support the more lightly armed versions.

(**Above**) The crew of a Panther *Befehlswagen* or command vehicle pose in front of their vehicle in the summer of 1944. These Panthers were purely designed to give a tank unit commander mobility and communications on the battlefield.

(**Opposite, above**) A Panther Ausf.G rolls through a town during operations in the summer of 1944. The '102' painted on the turret side identifies this tank as the I Abteilung Stab deputy commander or 'AD'. Since only the first three tanks in the battalion headquarters have command radios, this commander will have to give it up to the battalion commanding officer if the latter's Panther '101' is damaged.

(**Opposite, below**) Two heavily camouflaged Panther Ausf.Gs in a Normandy village in July 1944. These Panthers possibly belong to the Panzer Lehr Division which was in the Normandy area at this time. On 10 June 1944 the division reported a strength of ninety-eight Pz.Kpfw.IVs and eighty-eight Panthers. However, within a month the division had suffered heavy losses and had only forty-one Pz.Kpfw.IVs and thirty-six Panthers remaining.

I02

A Pz.Kpfw.IV Ausf.J with an Sd.Kfz.251/3 Ausf.C on the Eastern Front during Bagration in the summer of 1944.

An officer confers with two of his men standing next to a stationary Panther during early autumn operations on the Eastern Front.

An interesting photograph showing the rear of a well camouflaged Panther passing another Panther moving in a different direction during operations on the Western Front in the summer of 1944. In total there were 409 Panthers in the field in Normandy in June. On 7 June the Pz.Kpfw.IV and Panthers of the 12th SS Panzer Division 'Hitlerjugend' and the 21st Panzer Division fought a number of offensive and then defensive actions in Normandy.

A well camouflaged Panther moving along a forested road in northern France. By 7 June 1944 Panther tanks were soon embroiled in heavy fighting in the Normandy sector against the Allies.

Three excellent photographs taken in sequence showing a heavily camouflaged Panther Ausf.G with mounted Panzergrenadiers hitching a lift as the tank rolls through a French village during the summer of 1944. Note the third photograph with the Panther pulling alongside another Panther Ausf.G. For the defence of France there were initially only two Panther-equipped Panzer regiments on the Western Front, with a total of 156 Panthers. However, in a status report dated 30 July 1944, from June through August 1944 an additional seven Panther regiments were sent into France, reaching a maximum strength of 432.

Two camouflaged Ausf.G Panther tanks operating in France during the summer of 1944. In Normandy the Panther was often deployed to ambush positions in woods and scored a high kill rate against Allied armour. Although the Panthers were virtually wiped out in Normandy, its units conducted bitter offensive and then defensive fighting, often holding back the enemy for some time.

Two Panther crews resting in a wooded clearing with their tanks. While the Panther battalions scored a number of successes in Normandy in the summer of 1944, the tank was poorly suited for hedgerow terrain because of its width. Its long gun barrel also reduced manoeuvrability especially in the small villages and forest fighting.

The crew of this Panther Ausf.G rest beside their vehicle during a pause in their march across France in the summer of 1944. Losses of the Panther had been high due to the vulnerability to side and close-in attacks in the built-up areas of towns and villages in Normandy. *Bocage* combat for the battalions was not much better for the Panther either.

A Panther passes through a decimated French village during operations in Normandy in the summer of 1944. Camouflaging the Panther was of the utmost importance as enemy air attack was a constant danger.

A Panther Ausf.A moving through a French village. The tank has received an application of anti-magnetic mine paste.

Wehrmacht soldiers can be seen standing around a stationary Panther Ausf.D in the summer of 1944.

(**Opposite**) A staged photograph showing a Panzer crewman standing next to his tank with one crewman on his left who is conversing with a Wehrmacht soldier in a Paris street, probably in August 1944. The paper the crewman is reading is the German daily Paris newspaper that was distributed to German occupation troops.

A late Panther Ausf.G advances through a battered town during operations in September 1944. This tank belongs to a Panzer Regiment I battalion, 3rd Company, second vehicle of the second platoon, as identified by the tactical markings '322' painted in either black or red on the turret side.

PARISER ZEITUNG

432

(**Opposite, above**) A Panther Ausf.A in late summer 1944. Note the German transport truck on the left transporting horses. Even by this period of the war with newer, bigger and more powerful armoured vehicles being introduced on the front lines, draught animals were still used extensively by the Germans both on the Western and Eastern Fronts.

(**Opposite, below**) A Panther being directed onto a dirt road by a crew member. Note that one of its side skirts is missing, more than likely lost during an enemy contact.

(**Above**) A stationary well camouflaged Panther in the late summer of 1944. Through September and October a series of new Panzer brigades equipped with Panther tanks were sent into France to try to stop the Allied advance with counter-attacks. However, these newly formed Panther units were poorly trained and tactically disorganised and as a result were virtually wiped out.

Chapter Four

The Last Year of the War (1944–45)

On the Western Front in France, the military situation was also equally dire for the Germans. When the Allies attacked along the shore of the Normandy coast in early June 1944, there were initially only two Panther-equipped Panzer regiments established on the Western Front, with a total of 156 Panthers between them. From June to August 1944, an additional seven Panther regiments were sent into France, reaching a maximum strength of 432 tanks.

One Panzer Division to receive large numbers of Panthers for the defence of Normandy was the 12th SS 'Hitlerjugend'. It consisted of a standard SS Panzer Regiment, a Panther-equipped battalion and one Pz.Kpfw.IV-equipped tank battalion. By the time the Allies had brought ashore their troops, the 12SS had eighty-one Panthers, mainly Ausf.G variants, waiting for them inland. Though the tank crews were often inexperienced due to their age, they were fanatically motivated, making them relentless opponents. The 12SS fought a bloody defensive action, with Panther tanks being used to ambush the enemy in woods or undergrowth.

Alongside the Hitlerjugend division, another Waffen-SS armoured formation was equally engaged in defensive fighting: the 2nd SS Panzer Division 'Das Reich'. This division contained one of the most famous tank aces of the war: an SS NCO named Ernest Barkmann. Barkmann had already earned a reputation for his use of Panther tanks during bitter defensive fighting on the Eastern Front in late 1943. In Normandy he commanded the Ausf.G Panzers of the famous 4th Company, 2nd SS Panzer Regiment and scored an extraordinarily high kill rate against British and American armoured formations. However, not even his skill and doggedness could slow the unavoidable worsening of the German front line in Normandy.

In an effort to halt the Allied advance, a number of Panzer brigades were up-armoured and equipped with Panthers. But the Panther units were newly formed, poorly trained and tactically disorganised, and suffered heavy losses.

Following the disintegration of German resistance in France, the Allies advanced into Belgium and approached the borders of the Reich itself. At this point, Hitler decided to surprise his commanders by ordering a massive counteroffensive on the Western Front, known as the Ardennes Offensive.

A month before this, the German High Command rapidly built up their badly weakened Panzerwaffe with their elite Waffen-SS Panzer Divisions who would spearhead the attack. Four SS divisions were assigned to advance through the Ardennes: 1st SS Panzer Division 'Leibstandarte', 2nd SS Panzer Division 'Das Reich', 9th SS Panzer Division 'Hohenstaufen' and the 12th SS Panzer Division 'Hitlerjugend'. Each of these divisions consisted of one organic armoured battalion, each with a mixture of Pz.Kpfw.IV and Panther tanks, about ninety-five each. The 'Das Reich' deployed fifty-eight Panthers and the 'Hohenstaufen' thirty-five. This was considered to be well under strength. But the Germans believed their Panthers were superior to the Sherman and all other tanks.

The offensive initially went well, with the Panther once again demonstrating its prowess in open country, where it could hit its targets at long range with near impunity. However, the tank units were vulnerable in the close quarter fighting in the small towns and villages of the Ardennes where they suffered heavy losses. By 15 January 1945 it was reported that only ninety-seven operational Panthers were left in the units involved in the operation out of an initial strength of 282.

By the second week of January 1945 it was clear that the Ardennes offensive had failed and Hitler had lost his last gamble in the west.

On the Eastern Front the situation was no better. During the last months of 1944, there was a frantic attempt by the Panzerwaffe to stem the rout of the Soviet drive into Poland. Between June and September 1944 the Germans had sustained some one million casualties. To make good their losses many of the exhausted divisions were re-manned with conscripted old men and low-grade troops. This method of recruitment generally did not produce very good results. Also the numbers were insufficient, and the supply of volunteers into the German army was beginning to dry up. There was not time to train new Panzerwaffe crews properly and losses soared. Lack of fuel, spare parts and trained crews all played their part in reducing the effectiveness of the Panther battalions in the final year of the war, and the Russians continued pushing forward while German forces retreated through Poland.

By early February 1945 German forces in the East had been driven back across Poland to the River Oder, the last bastion of defence before Berlin. Only three weeks earlier the Eastern Front had been still deep in Poland. Now Upper Silesia was lost; in East Prussia German forces were smashed to pieces; West Prussia and Pomerania were being defended by depleted troops thrown together; and the defence of the Oder was now being entrusted to exhausted armies that had been fighting for months in Poland along the Vistula. What was left of these forces were supposed to hold the Oder front and fight to the death.

In Hungary too, where Hitler had been eager to stem the Russian drive, overwhelming Soviet forces had steadily driven the elite Sixth SS Panzer Army from Budapest, leaving a trail of destruction. In fact, fighting had been so futile that the

12th SS Panzer Division 'Hitlerjugend', which had received forty-four Panzers including sixteen new Panther Ausf.Gs, lost thirty-five Panthers during operations in Hungary.

Elsewhere on the Eastern Front, the few Panthers that were left in the field were thrown into ad hoc units for the final desperate efforts of defending the front lines. When the Russians finally attacked the Oder in mid-April 1945, there was still one complete Panther battalion left. The battalion went on to undertake successful defensive measures in spite overwhelming opposition. However, within days the Russians carved its way across the Oder River, capturing the town of Küstrin/Kostrzyn and heading towards the Nazi capital.

As the Russians poured down the Berlin highway the III SS Panzer Corps were given the task of scraping together enough armoured vehicles including Panthers, Tigers and Panzerjäger to defend the line on the 3rd Panzer Army's flank along the Finow Canal. Although these formations fought bitterly to defend the capital from the advancing Red Army, the Russians systematically built a great encirclement of steel and fire around the city, surrounding it completely by 24 April. Berlin was doomed, but even during the battle on 26 April the commander of the 503rd heavy tank battalion was able to report that he still had six tanks ready for active service to defend the routes leading into Berlin. This was hardly enough tanks to stem the mighty Red Army, but even so courageous Panther and Tiger crews fought on ceaselessly to prolong the death throes of the Panzerwaffe.

During the last days of the war most of the remaining Panzer divisions continued to fight as a unit until they were destroyed and their equipment surrendered. The Panther, though it had been a deadly adversary to the enemy, had been introduced into the war too late. Nobody could deny that the men of the Panther battalions, in their brief existence, had shown extraordinary daring and professionalism in combat. The Panzerwaffe and the Panzergrenadiers had provided Germany with the backbone of its defence, and in doing so had been destroyed.

Two Panthers moving through a town on the Western Front in 1944. The Panther battalions demonstrated their prowess in open country, where they could hit targets at long range with near-impunity. However in small towns the Panthers suffered heavy losses, and the *bocage* with its thick hedges also presented problems.

A Panther Ausf.A advancing across a bridging section during operations in the summer of 1944. Note how the engineers have chocked the bridge with large wooden blocks for support.

Panther tanks can be seen being transported on special flat-bed railway cars to the front. Both vehicles have a full application of Zimmerit anti-magnetic mine paste.

A command Panther Ausf.A during operations in the summer of 1944. A battalion command contained a communication and reconnaissance platoon of three Befehlswagen Panthers and a reconnaissance platoon of five Panthers often supported by Sd.Kfz.251 halftracks and Sd.Kfz.234 'Pumas'.

A13

(**Opposite, above**) A column of Panthers advancing along a road bound for the front lines.

(**Opposite, below**) A crewman poses with his Panther Ausf.D sitting on the tank's powerful 7.5cm KwK L/70 gun. The tank man's uniform insignia are unclear, but they seem to indicate an SS unit. The large tactical 'A13' in red with white outline is interesting: the letter may indicate either O Abteilung or 1 Kompanie of this unidentified regiment.

(**Above**) A Panther can be seen operating near some buildings during operations on the Western Front in 1944. Only two Panther-equipped Panzer regiments initially operated on the Western Front, with a total of 156 Panthers between them. However, from June to August 1944, an additional seven Panther regiments were sent into France, reaching a maximum strength of 432.

(**Opposite, above**) This photograph appears to have been taken during operations in Italy in 1944. It shows a Jagdpanzer 38 or Hetzer 38(t) and a Panther advancing together along a road inside a town. The Jagdpanzer 38 first entered service in July 1944 and would eventually be assigned to either an infantry unit or a Panzerjäger or Volksgrenadier division. The Hetzer would go on to assist and support Panther units during the latter part of the war in an anti-tank role.

(**Opposite, below**) A Volkswagen 166 Schwimmwagen from III Abteilung SS Panzergrenadier Regiment 'Germania' approaching an Sd.Kfz.251/1 halftrack from the same unit. Behind that is a Panther tank from the 5 Kompanie SS Panzer-Regiment 5.

(**Above**) An interesting photograph showing Panzergrenadiers hitching a lift on board a Panther Ausf.G from Panzer-Brigade 109 during operations in Hungary in 1944. During 1944 ten new Panzer brigades were formed and each was organised with thirty-three Panthers in a Panzer-Abteilung.

(**Above**) Another second-generation tank destroyer to make its debut in 1944 was the Jagdpanther or 'hunting Panther', pictured in this photograph being put through trials. The vehicle boasted a lethal 8.8cm KwK 43 cannon which was originally fitted on the new Tiger II and mounted on a Panther chassis. This unturreted tank destroyer had thick armoured sloped hull sides, and inside the hull was a roomy interior. For local defence it was armed with an MG34 machine gun fitted in a ball mount on the right side of the front glacis plate. There were two main variants manufactured: the first produced was the earlier 1944 G1 model with a small internally bolted main gun mantlet and a modified Panther A engine deck. The later variant, built later in 1944, was known as the G2, which had a larger outside-bolted mantlet and a modified Panther G engine deck.

(**Opposite**) Two photographs showing Jagdpanthers during operations in France in the summer of 1944. The Jagdpanthers served in the heavy anti-tank battalions or Schwere Panzerjäger-Abteilungen and operated mainly in Russia. They were also seen operating in small numbers in July 1944 in Normandy where the German 654th Heavy Anti-tank Battalion deployed about twelve Jagdpanthers against British units. Months later in the Ardennes in December 1944 there were larger numbers that fought against American units. The success of the Jagdpanther, though limited in numbers, prompted the introduction of the Jagdtiger or 'Hunting Tiger' onto the battlefield.

CAFE
BILLARD

Another photograph showing a Jagdpanther during operations in France in the summer of 1944.

(**Opposite, above**) Panzergrenadiers have hitched a lift aboard a Panther during operations in the summer of 1944. This Panzer belongs to the 31st Panzer Regiment of the 5th Panzer Division. In its operations on the Eastern Front the division was seen as one of the best German units by their Soviet counterparts. It was almost destroyed during the Russian summer offensive in 1944, but continued to defend and fight until April 1945.

(**Opposite, below**) A Panther crewman belonging to 'Totenkopf' Division can be seen standing next to his Panther Ausf.G in 1944. The division in 1944 was attached to the IV SS Panzer Korps. Following the collapse of German Army Group Centre in August 1944 the corps was placed into the line around Warsaw where it saw extensive action against strong Soviet forces. Elements of the corps took part in the suppression of the Warsaw uprising, but were slowly pushed back to the area near Modlin, where it fought until December.

431

A Panther Ausf.A can be seen advancing along a dusty road probably in August 1944. This Panther belongs to the 'Totenkopf' Division of the I./SS-Panzer Regiment 3. From the summer of 1944, the Abteilung fought in Siedlice and later in the defensive battles around Warsaw. Later in 1945 the Abteilung was to take part in the Konrad operations in Hungary to relieve the forces trapped inside Budapest.

A Panther in Poland in the summer of 1944. By this period of the war the Panzer battalions were hard pressed to contain the advancing Russians. As a result of the high losses, the Panthers were replaced or supported by Pz.Kpfw.IVs and Sturmgeschütz IIIs.

A Panther being resupplied with ammunition in 1944. All the ammunition for the main armament was stored in the hull, much of it in the sponsons. For all models, three rounds were kept under the turntable of the turret.

A well camouflaged Panther with foliage covering much of the vehicle during a defensive action in the summer of 1944. Note the logs attached to the turret sides. It looks as if the crew have used these logs for additional protection; however its more likely that they were to be used for traction if the tank were to become stuck in the mud.

A Panther that has evidently developed a mechanical problem is being towed by two Sd.kfz.9s, also known as 'Famos'. The Famo, found in all the Panther battalions, could tow some 28 tonnes. This was more than adequate for medium tanks like the Pz.Kpfw.IV, but two or even three or four were necessary for heavier vehicles like the Tiger I, King Tiger and Panther, as this photograph illustrates. It also towed an Sd.Anh.116 low-loader trailer to carry disabled vehicles. These halftracks were equipped with a winch mounted at the middle of the vehicle just under the cargo platform.

A Panther Ausf.G during operations on the Eastern Central Front. During the early summer of 1944 the Germans had considerably reinforced their strength on the Central Front with armoured vehicles. During this period various armoured units were furnished with additional Panthers. Mixed units like the I/Pz.Rgt 'Brandenburg' assigned to the Panzergrenadier Division 'Kurmark' now had forty-five Panthers, while Pz.Rgt 29 (Pz. Div. 'Münchenberg') had twenty-one Ausf.As.

The first of five photographs taken in sequence showing a column of Panthers from the 1st Panzer Regiment 27 of the 19th Panzer Division during operations in Poland in the summer of 1944. The division was almost destroyed in early 1944 during a number of defensive battles and was sent to the Netherlands in May 1944 to be refitted. Following the Russian summer offensive, which almost destroyed German Army Group Centre, the division was sent by rail from the Netherlands back to the Eastern Front. It took part in the defence of Warsaw and the crushing of the Polish uprising.

A Panther tank rolls along a road during operations on the Eastern Front. A prime mover can be seen passing the other way hauling a 15cm howitzer.

A photograph of Panther II02 belonging to Panzer-Regiment 3 of the SS 'Totenkopf' Division which was part of the advanced elements fighting alongside the 'Wiking' Division during this period east of Warsaw in the summer of 1944.

During operations east of Warsaw in August 1944 and a Panther tank belonging to 8.Kompanie SS Panzer-Regiment 5 and a halftrack from the III Abteilung SS Panzergrenadier Regiment 9 'Germania'. Standing between the vehicles is Hauptsturmführer Karl Nicolussi-Leck. He was commander of the 2.Kompanie 5.SS Panzer Abteilung.

Two vehicles to be found in a Panther battalion were the Sd.Kfz.251 halftrack personnel carrier and the Pz.Kpfw IV tank, both pictured in this photograph advancing across a field on the Eastern Front.

(**Above**) Out on the Eastern Front halted in a field are a number of Sd.Kfz.251 halftrack personnel carriers. These have been purposely spaced apart to reduce the risk of an aerial attack.

(**Opposite**) A Wehrmacht soldier, more than likely a motorcyclist, wearing the rubberised motorcycle greatcoat. He can be seen looking across a road at a Panther tank during the Warsaw Uprising in August 1944.

(**Below**) A Panther advancing along a track during operations in the summer of 1944 in Poland. Following the Russian Offensive, Operation Bagration, in June and July 1944, the German army never recovered from the material and manpower losses sustained by the massive Soviet attack. The offensive was so damaging that what was left of Army Group Centre withdrew into Poland and took up defensive positions there instead. Included were a number of Panther battalions.

A Waffen-SS crew posing with their Ausf.G or H Pz.Kpfw.IV in Warsaw in August 1944. These tanks supported the Panther on the battlefield until the end of the war.

A Panther Ausf.G rolls along a snowy road during the Ardennes operation in late 1944. The continuous fighting on the Western Front gradually took its toll on the tracks and other moving parts of the Panther. Those that survived fought a desperate defensive action all the way back to Germany.

(**Opposite, above**) A column of whitewashed Panthers somewhere on the Eastern Front in late 1944. By this period of the war German forces in the east were bitterly defending Upper Silesia, East and West Prussia and Pomerania. All of these lines were being defended by depleted troops thrown together with ad hoc armoured units comprising a motley collection of Panthers, Tigers, Pz.Kpfw.IVs and other vehicles.

(**Opposite, below**) A Panther Ausf.G from the 1/SS Panzer-Regiment 1 of the 1.SS Panzer Division 'LSSAH' photographed during its operations in Hungary in February or March 1945.

(**Above**) Panzergrenadiers hitching a lift onboard a Panther as it advances along a road somewhere on the Eastern Front in late 1944.

(**Opposite, above**) A photograph taken from a Panther showing a Panzer unit advancing across the snow in a 'V' formation. Note an old Pz.kpfw.III command tank (Panzerbefehlswagen III) supporting the drive.

(**Opposite, below**) Two Panther Ausf.Gs can be seen advancing along a road during operations in the Alsace in January 1945. These tanks belong to the 10th SS Panzer Division 'Frundsberg'. On 3 January 1945 the 10.SS-Panzer-Regiment 'Langemarck' increased to two battalions, including creating one Panther battalion with four companies and one Pz.Kpfw.IV battalion with three companies.

(**Above**) Various vehicles can be seen outside a Russian village in late 1944. A column of Sd.Kfz.251 armoured personnel carriers is passing through the village past two stationary Pz.Kpfw.IVs. The halftrack, especially the Sd.Kfz.251, was a very versatile vehicle and could travel across some of the most rugged terrain. It was seen in every Panther battalion until the end of the war.

(**Above**) During operations in late 1944 early 1945 and a halftrack Sd.Kfz.251 is towing a light Horch cross-country vehicle across a muddy field. A VW Kübelwagen is following the other two vehicles. All three were to be found in a Panther battalion.

(**Opposite, above**) An interesting photograph showing an Sd.Kfz.10/5 parked by the side of a road. This is the unarmoured version mounting the 2cm FlaK 38, although the identifying feature was not the gun but the width of the platform. These vehicles were issued to independent anti-aircraft battalions in both the Heer and Luftwaffe. They also supported both Tiger and Panther battalions during the later part of the war.

(**Opposite, below**) A Panther Ausf.A rolling along a street in Hungary during in February or March 1945. It was in Hungary that German strategy placed the utmost importance on defending what was regarded as the last bastion of defence in the East. Against all military logic, the Germans felt that it was Hungary and not the Vistula River in Poland which presented a natural barrier against an advance on Germany. For the defence of Hungary the Germans sent their premier Waffen-SS divisions, including 'Totenkopf' and 'Wiking'. This meant drawing off important armour, including many Panthers.

(**Above**) Waffen-SS commanding officers can be seen inside a Volkswagen Schwimmwagen during operations in Hungary in January 1944. Behind them are two Panthers negotiating the uneven terrain.

(**Opposite, above**) A column of vehicles including an Sd.Kfz.251, support trucks and a Panther can be seen on a road during operations in Hungary in 1945.

(**Opposite, below**) An abandoned late model Jagdpanther in early 1945. This vehicle has more than likely fallen in to Russian hands; note the Soviet 'G' painted on the glacis.

(**Above**) An Sd.Kfz.234/3 and a 5cm Sd.Kfz.234/2 on a training ground in 1944. These vehicles were often found in Panther battalions and used for reconnaissance duties.

(**Opposite, above**) A 5cm Sd.Kfz.234/2 heavily camouflaged, more than likely operating on the Western Front in 1944. These 'Puma' vehicles were used in reconnaissance units and often provided the Panther battalions with flak or anti-tank support.

(**Opposite, below**) An Sd.Kfz.234 seen here operating in France in 1944. These vehicles were found in heavy reconnaissance battalions and consisted of various self-propelled anti-tank gun mountings, both wheeled and half-tracked. The battalion was fully equipped with radio vehicles comprising Sd.Kfz.250/3s with the primary task of transmitting data during reconnaissance missions. During these missions, which were often hazardous and costly in men and equipment, the battalion had Panzergrenadier support for armoured car or armoured reconnaissance company operations. The Sd.Kfz.234 supported these missions due to its versatility, speed and firepower and assisted the Panther battalions in the field.

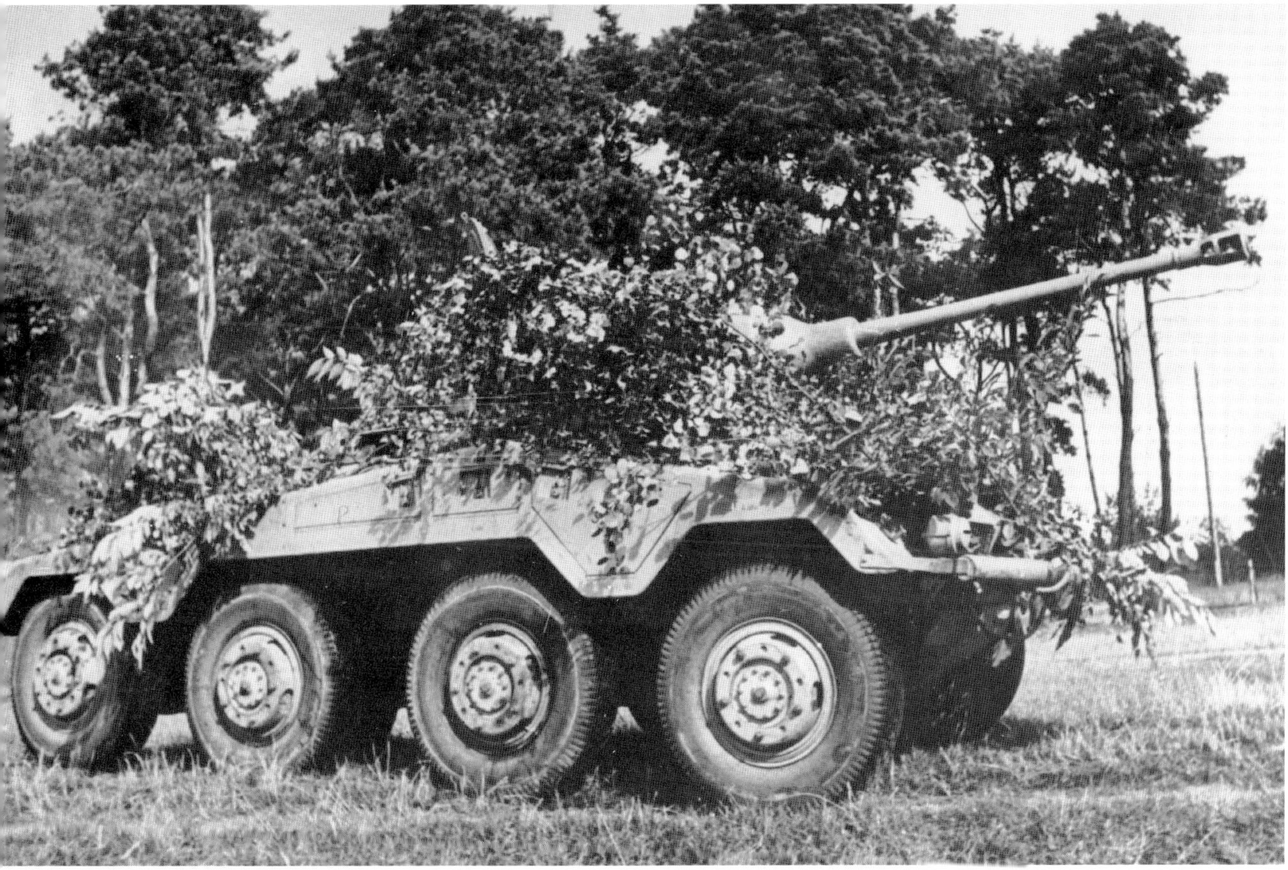

Four photographs showing various Panthers knocked out or abandoned by their crew. By January 1945 production of the Panther tank had reduced considerably, and eight of the Panther regiments still on the Western Front were transferred to the Eastern Front in February 1945. The result was that, for the rest of the war, the greatest threats to tanks were no longer German tanks but infantry anti-tank weapons and tank destroyers. The Panthers fought on but were eventually destroyed by enemy anti-tank fire or ran out of fuel and were abandoned.

The last bastion of defence. In this photograph a Panther turret defensive position in one of the main streets in Berlin in May 1945. Note the discarded shells around the position.

Appendix I

Panther Tank Specification

Dimensions

Length: 8.86 m (29 ft 1 in) including gun, 6.87 m (22 ft 6 in) hull only
Width: 3.27 m (10 ft 9 in) hull, 3.42 m (11 ft 3 in) with skirt plates
Height: 2.99 m (9 ft 10 in)
Combat weight: 44.8 tonnes (99,000 lbs)

Suspension and tracks

Type: dual torsion bar
Shock absorbers: on 2nd and 7th swing arms on either side
Track type: Kgs 64/660/150 dual centre guide
Track width: 660 mm (26 in)
Ground contact length: 3.92 m (12 ft 10 in)
Track links: 86
Ground pressure: 0.86 kg/cm^2

Engine and transmission

Maybach HL 230 P30 V-12, four-stroke internal combustion
Displacement: 23.095 litres (1,409.3in^3)
Compression ratio: 6.8:1
Fuel: petrol, 74 octane
Power: 700 metric horsepower (690 hp) at 3,000 rpm
Fuel consumption: 3.5 l/km (0.81 mpg (Imp), 0.67 mpg (US)) on road
Fuel capacity: 730 l (160 gal (Imp); 190 gal (US))
Transmission: ZF AK 7-200 synchromesh manual coupled through Fichtel & Sachs LAG 3/70H clutchgears, 7 forward, 1 reverse
Steering: MAN single-radius clutch-brake
Steering ratio: 1:1.5

Armour

Hull front, lower: 60 mm (2.4 in) at 35°; upper: 80 mm (3.1 in) at 35°; (Ausf.G: lower hull front reduced to 50 mm)
Hull side, lower: 40 mm (1.6 in) at 90°; upper: 40 mm at 50°; (Ausf.G: upper hull side changed to 50 mm at 60°)

Hull rear: 40 mm at 60°
Turret front: 100 mm at 78°
Turret side: 45 mm at 65°
Turret rear: 45 mm at 65°
Turret, top: 16 mm at 5°
Gun mantlet: 100 mm, rounded

Armament
Main gun: 7.5 cm KwK 42 L/70
Turret traverse rate: 24°/second
Elevation: +18°/−8°
Rounds carried: 79; Ausf.G: 82
Primary gun sight: Leitz TZF 12; Ausf.A and G: TZF 12a
Magnification: 2.5 × /5 ×
Field of view: 28°/14°
Radio equipment: Fu 5 transmitter/receiver/Fu 2 receiver

Performance
Road speed: 55 km/h (34 mph) at 3,000 rpm with HL 230 engine
Road range: 200 km (120 miles)

Obstacle crossing
Vertical obstacle: 0.9 m
Trench crossing: 2.45 m
Fording: 1.9 m

Appendix II

Panther Variants (1943–45)

Ausf.D

First production series manufactured by MAN, Daimler-Benz, MNH and Henschel. 850 built between January and September 1943.

Ausf.A

The second production series manufactured by MAN, Daimler-Benz, Demag and MNH. 2,000 built between August 1943 and May 1944.

Ausf.G

The third production series manufactured by MAN, Daimler-Benz, MNH. 3,126 built between March 1944 and April 1945.

Panzerbefehlswagen mit 7.5cm KwK 42 L/70. Panzerkampfwagen Panther (Sd.Kfz.171) (als Pz.Bef.Wg.) / Panzerbefehlswagen Panther Ausf.A (Sd.Kfz.267)

329 converted with extra radio equipment and reduced ammunition storage.

Panzerbeobachtswagen Panther

Artillery observation tank converted from Panther I by removing the main armament and fitting a dummy gun with a ball fitting for a machine gun on the blanked-off turret front. Forty-one were converted late 1944-early 1945.

Jagdpanther (Sd.Kfz.173). Panzerjäger für 8.8cm PaK43 auf Fahrgestell Panther I

Tank destroyers based on the Panther chassis mounted with a 8.8cm PaK43 L/71 fitted to a fixed superstructure in a limited traverse mounting. 392 built by MIAG and MNH from January 1944 to March 1945.

Panzer-Bergegerät (Panther I) (Sd.Kfz.179). Bergepanther

Armoured recovery vehicles using the Panther I chassis. 347 built or converted by Henschel, MAN and Demag.

Appendix III

Composition of a Panzer Reconnaissance Grenadier Battalion (1943–44)

The Panzer Reconnaissance Battalion, mid-1943

Battalion Headquarters (5 officers, 22 men); Communications Platoon (1 officer, 60 men); Train and Maintenance (6 officers, 87 men); Heavy Armoured Car Platoon (1 officer, 21 men).

Heavy Company (5 officers, 199 men)

Company HQ (1 officer, 15 men); Anti-tank Platoon (1 officer, 36 men); Infantry Gun Platoon (1 officer, 24 men); Pioneer Platoon (1 officer, 58 men); Cannon Platoon (1 officer, 37 men); Company Train and Maintenance (29 men).

Armoured Car Company (4 officers, 114 men)

Company Headquarters (1 officer, 9 men); Heavy Platoon (2 officers, 22 men); Three Light Platoons (*each* 1 officer *or* NCO, 17 men); Train and Maintenance (30 men).

Armoured Car Company (3 officers, 110 men)

Company Headquarters (1 officer, 10 men); Four Platoons (*each* 1 officer *or* NCO, 17 men); Train and Maintenance (30 men).

Light Column (1 officer, 50 men)

Column HQ (1 officer, 14 men); Detachment (11 men); Two Detachments (*each* 9 men); Train (7 men).

Two Light Armoured Rifle Companies (3 officers, 233 men), *each* consisted of:

Company Headquarters (1 officer, 12 men); Train and Maintenance (30 men); Heavy Platoon consisted of Platoon HQ (1 officer, 5 men), Mortar Group (18 men), Two Heavy Machine Gun Groups (*each* 17 men); Three Rifle Platoons, *each* consisted of Platoon HQ (1 officer *or* NCO, 8 men), Three Rifle Squads (*each* 12 men).

Total Strength of 1,161 all ranks (32 officers and 1,129 men)

The Panzer Reconnaissance Battalion, c.1944

Battalion Headquarters (4 officers, 19 men); Communications Platoon (1 officer, 54 men); Train and Maintenance (17 men); Heavy Armoured Car Platoon (1 officer, 21 men).

Heavy Company (5 officers and 185 men)

Company Headquarters (1 officer, 15 men); Infantry Gun Platoon (1 officer, 24 men); Pioneer Platoon (1 officer, 53 men); Cannon Platoon (1 officer, 34 men); Anti-tank Platoon (1 officer, 31 men); Train and Maintenance (28 men).

Armoured Car Company (3 officers and 114 men)

Company Headquarters (1 officer, 9 men); Heavy Platoon (1 officer, 23 men); Three Light Platoons, (*each* 1 officer *or* NCO, 17 men); Train and Maintenance (29 men).

Armoured Car Company 'C' (3 officers, 108 men)

Company Headquarters (1 officer, 9 men); Four Platoons (*each* 1 officer *or* NCO, 17 men); Train and Maintenance (29 men).

Supply Company (6 officers, 107 men)

Company Headquarters (1 officer, 9 men); Train (9 men); Maintenance Detachment (3 officers, 36 men); Fuel Detachment (18 men); Munitions Detachment (14 men); Supply Detachment (1 officer, 12 men); Medical Detachment (1 officer, 5 men); Company Train (4 men).

Two Armoured Reconnaissance Companies (3 officers, 194 men)

Each consisted of Company Headquarters (1 officer, 16 men); Train and Maintenance (30 men); Mortar Group (18 men); Three Rifle Platoons, *each* consisted of Platoon HQ (1 officer *or* NCO, 7 men), Three Rifle Squads (*each* 12 men).

Total Strength of 1,042 all ranks (29 officers and 1,013 men)

Armoured Composition of the Battalion

Battalion Headquarters

This consisted of the Battalion Commander, Adjutant, ordnance and medical officers, equipped with two halftracks and additional cars and motorcycles.

Platoon HQ

The Platoon HQ was divided between two vehicles. The first was normally a 250/1, the second a 250/10 which mounted a 3.7cm Pak cannon for additional fire support. In late 1943 the 3.7cm Pak was replaced on a number of vehicles with the much more powerful 7.5cm. Additional fire support came from the Heavy Platoon which operated four Sd.Kfz.250/7s that mounted an 8cm mortar on each. There were also three 250/1 vehicles each consisting of a group of heavy machine gunners armed with two MG34 or MG42 teams.

Company HQ

Used two Sd.Kfz.250/3 command vehicles plus four or five motorcycles, and as ever there was the Train and Maintenance team for supply and repair duties.

Communications Platoon

Maintained radio and line communications within the Battalion.

Heavy Armoured Car Platoon

A variety of vehicles including the Sd.Kfz.233. The platoon normally fielded six of these vehicles.

Armoured Car Company

Equipped with three Sd.Kfz.231 and three Sd.Kfz.232 vehicles, eight-wheeled, each with a four-man crew. The three Light Platoons used four Sd.Kfz.222 and two Sd.Kfz.223 armoured.

Armoured Car Company 'C'

The second Armoured Car Company used the Sd.Kfz.250. Four platoons each operated two commanded versions, the 250/5 equipped as a radio car, and four gun versions, the 250/9 mounting a 2cm cannon.

The Rifle Company

This company operated the Sd.Kfz.250 halftrack with a squad of twelve men, a leader and an assistant. Both vehicles carried their own machine pistol and light machine gun.

The Panzer Reconnaissance Battalion, mid-1944

Battalion Headquarters (4 officers, 18 men).

Staff Company (3 officers, 113 men)

Company HQ (1 officer, 11 men); Communications Platoon (1 officer, 43 men); Two Heavy Armoured Car Platoons (*each* 1 officer *or* NCO, 23 men); Cannon Group (12 men).

Supply Company (7 officers, 202 men)

Company HQ (2 officers, 16 men); Medical Detachment (1 officer, 4 men); Maintenance Detachment (3 officers, 112 men); Fuel Detachment (16 men); Munitions Detachment (13 men); Supply Detachment (1 officer, 41 men).

Heavy Company (4 officers, 150 men)

Company HQ (1 officer, 14 men); Cannon Platoon (1 officer, 31 men); Pioneer Platoon (1 officer, 50 men); 8cm Mortar Platoon (1 officer, 55 men).

Armoured Car Company (3 officers, 82 men)

Company HQ (1 officer, 12 men); Four Platoons (*each* 1 officer *or* NCO, 17 men).

Light Reconnaissance Company (3 officers, 164 men)

Company HQ (1 officer, 17 men); Mortar Group (17 men); Cannon Group (9 men); Three Rifle Platoons, *each* consisted of Platoon HQ (1 officer *or* NCO, 4 men), Three Rifle Squads (*each* 12 men).

Heavy Reconnaissance Company (3 officers, 180 men)

Company HQ (1 officer, 17 men); Heavy Platoon consisted of Platoon HQ (1 officer, 8 men), Mortar Group (15 men), Cannon Group (8 men), Two Heavy Machine Gun Groups (*each* 11 men), Three Rifle Platoons, *each* consisted of Platoon HQ (1 officer *or* NCO, 6 men), Three Rifle Squads (*each* 10 men).

Total Strength of 936 all ranks (23 officers and 913 men)

Armoured Composition of the Battalion

Heavy Armoured Car Platoon

Now part of the HQ Company with each platoon fielding six Sd.Kfz.234/1 heavy armoured cars, some of which mounted either a 5cm gun or 7.5cm Pak 40.

Cannon Group

Consisted of three Sd.Kfz.234/3, mounting the 7.5cm cannon.

Pioneer Platoon

Its three squads were fifteen strong and were transported in two Sd.Kfz.251/7 pioneer halftracks.

8cm Mortar Platoon

Had six Sd.Kfz.251/2 halftracks each mounting an 8cm mortar, with an additional Sd.kfz.251 for Platoon HQ.

Armoured Car Company

Equipped with three Sd.Kfz.231 and three Sd.Kfz.232 vehicles, again eight-wheeled, each with a four-man crew. The three Light Platoons used four Sd.Kfz.222 and two Sd.Kfz.223 armoured.

The Rifle Company

This company operated the Sd.Kfz.250 halftrack with a squad of twelve men, a leader and an assistant. Both vehicles carried their own machine pistol and light machine gun.

The Mortar Group

Two Sd.Kfz.250/8 and a 250/1 for munitions.

The Panzer Grenadier Battalion, 1943

Battalion Headquarters (5 officers, 16 men); Communications Platoon (24 men); Battalion Train and Maintenance (5 officers, 60 men)

Heavy Company (5 officers, 199 men)

Company HQ (1 officer, 15 men); Anti-tank Platoon (1 officer, 36 men); Infantry Gun Platoon (1 officer, 24 men); Pioneer Platoon (1 officer, 58 men); Cannon Platoon (1 officer, 37 men); Company Train and Maintenance (29 men).

Three Rifle Companies (4 officers, 223 men)

Each consisted of Company HQ (1 officer, 13 men); Company Train and Maintenance (25 men); Heavy Platoon consisted of Platoon HQ (1 officer, 12 men), Mortar Group (16 men), Cannon Group (8 men), Two Heavy Machine Gun Groups, *each* (11 men); Three Rifle Platoons, *each* consisted of Platoon HQ (1 officer *or* NCO, 6 men), Three Rifle Squads (*each* 12 men).

Total Strength of 995 all ranks (27 officers and 968 men)

Armoured Composition of the Battalion

Battalion Headquarters

Consisted of the command staff of the Battalion with two halftracks, plus a number of field cars and motorcycles.

Communications Platoon

Consisted of a variety of vehicles for maintaining radio and line communications within the Battalion.

Anti-tank Platoon

Three Sd.Kfz.251 halftracks plus one Sd.Kkfz.250/1 for ammunition were used in a typical Panzer Grenadier Battalion. These were authorized to tow three 5cm or 3.7cm Paks. The lethal 7.5cm Pak 40 was also found in the platoon during 1943.

Infantry Gun Platoon

Three Sd.Kfz.251/4 halftracks towed 7.5cm infantry guns and also acted as ammunition carriers. There was an Sd.Kfz.251 at HQ.

Cannon Platoon

This fielded six self-propelled 7.5cm guns, each mounted on an Sd.Kfz.251/9 armoured halftrack, plus an HQ vehicle and ammunition carrier.

Pioneer Platoon

This consisted of three squads, each fifteen strong, with two light machine guns, carried in two Sd.Kfz.251/7 armoured halftracks. Platoon HQ was supported by an Sd.Kfz.251/10 with 3.7cm gun and an additional vehicle with flamethrower.

Heavy Anti-tank Rifle Platoon

This Anti-tank Rifle Platoon consisted of Sd.Kfz.250/11 halftracks towing the 2.8cm sPzB 41 anti-tank rifle grenade.

The Rifle Company

Consisted of Sd.Kfz.251/1 armoured halftracks carrying two gun teams, each with a gunner and loader, and four riflemen.

Heavy Platoon

Consisted of Sd.Kfz.251/2 armoured halftracks which were armed with 8cm mortars that were fired from the vehicle.

Platoon Headquarters

The Platoon Headquarters consisted of an Sdk.fz.251/9 or 10, which mounted its own 3.7cm Pak in place of a light machine gun. On some of the vehicles the 7.5cm infantry guns were mounted.

Company HQ

Was equipped with two Sd.Kfz.251/3 command halftracks.

The Panzer Grenadier Battalion, late 1943

Battalion Headquarters (6 officers, 20 men); Communications Platoon (1 officer, 22 men); Battalion Train and Maintenance (4 officers, 77 men).

Heavy Company (4 officers, 133 men)

Company HQ (1 officer, 16 men); Anti-tank Platoon (1 officer, 31 men); Infantry Gun Platoon (1 officer, 24 men); Cannon Platoon (1 officer, 34 men); Company Train and Maintenance (28 men).

Three Rifle Companies (3 officers, 217 men)

Each consisted of Company HQ (1 officer, 27 men); Company Train and Maintenance (25 men); Heavy Platoon consisted of Platoon HQ (1 officer, 10 men), Mortar Group (15 men), Cannon Group (8 men); Two Heavy Machine Gun Groups (*each* 11 men); Three Rifle Platoons, *each* consisted of Platoon HQ (1 officer *or* NCO, 6 men), Three Rifle Squads (*each* 10 men).

Total Strength of 927 all ranks (24 officers and 903 men)

The Panzer Grenadier Battalion, 1944

Battalion Headquarters (4 officers, 16 men); Communications Platoon (1 officer, 22 men).

Supply Company (7 officers, 156 men)

Company HQ (2 officers, 11 men); Medical Detachment (1 officer, 4 men); Maintenance Detachment (3 officers, 79 men); Fuel Detachment (12 men); Munitions Detachment (14 men); Supply Detachment (1 officer, 36 men).

Heavy Company (3 officers, 94 men)

Company HQ (1 officer, 18 men); Cannon Platoon (1 officer, 31 men); 12cm Mortar Platoon (1 officer, 45 men).

Three Rifle Companies (3 officers, 180 men)

Each consisted of Company HQ (1 officer, 17 men); Heavy Platoon consisted of Platoon HQ (1 officer, 8 men), Mortar Group (15 men), Cannon Group (8 men), Two Heavy Machine Gun Groups, *each* (11 men); Three Rifle Platoons, *each* consisted of Platoon HQ (1 officer *or* NCO, 6 men), Three Rifle Squads (*each* 10 men).

Total Strength of 852 all ranks (24 officers and 828 men)

Armoured Composition of the Battalion

Anti-tank Platoon

Three Sd.Kfz.251/17 halftracks, some mounting the 2cm anti-aircraft gun.

12cm Mortar Platoon

Consisted of Sd.Kfz.251/1, but the 12cm mortars were not fired from inside the vehicle. The platoon also contained an Sd.Kfz.250 ammunition carrier.

The Rifle Company

Consisted of a number of vehicles for personnel transportation and for carrying various equipment and ammunition. During late 1943 each squad was armed with its own 8.8cm Panzerschreck anti-tank launcher.

Platoon HQ

Consisted of the Sd.Kfz.251/17 armoured halftrack mounting its own 2cm Flak gun.

Heavy Platoon

Six Sd.Kfz.251/17 models were in one company. Towards the end of 1943 the Machine Gun Group vehicles along with the Platoon HQ machine were supposedly Sd.Kfz.251/17 models, for a total of six in the company. Each vehicle mounted a single machine gun team and was supported by a 2cm Flak gun crew.

The Panzer Battalion, c.1943

Battalion Headquarters (8 officers, 16 men)

Staff Company (6 officers, 250 men) (318 men in Panther Battalion)

Company HQ (1 officer, 3 men); Reconnaissance Platoon (1 officer, 24 men); Communication Platoon (1 officer, 17 men); Scout and Pioneer Platoon (1 officer, 52 men); Anti-aircraft Platoon (44 men); Train and Maintenance (2 officers, 110 men) (178 men in Panther Battalion).

Four Companies (3 officers, 158 men) (170 men in Panther Company)

Each consisted of Company HQ (1 officer, 13 men) (15 men in Panther Company); Trains and Maintenance (47 men) (58 men in Panther Company); Four Platoons, (*each* 1 officer *or* NCO and 24 men).

Total strength of 924 all ranks (26 officers and 898 men), or 1,030 men (26 officers and 1,014 men) in Panther Battalion.

Armoured Composition of the Battalion

Reconnaissance Platoon

Equipped mainly with five Panzer IV or Panther tanks.

Communication Platoon

Panzer III models or Panthers with three tanks.

Scout and Pioneer Platoon

Consisted of four motorcycle sections. Each of the ten men were carried on motorcycles or Kettenkrads, with a single light machine gun per section. The three pioneer sections were each nine-men strong, carried in an Sd.Kfz.251/7 with a halftrack or truck for equipment.

Anti-aircraft Platoon

Various halftracks were used in the platoon, occasionally mounted four 2cm cannons.

The Panzer Company

Equipped with twenty-two tanks, either Panzer IV or Panther.

The Panzer Battalion, mid-1944

Battalion Headquarters (4 officers, 10 men).

Staff Company (3 officers, 142 men)

Company HQ (1 officer, 4 men); Communication and Reconnaissance Platoon (1 officer, 45 men); Scout and Pioneer Platoon (1 officer, 53 men); Anti-aircraft Platoon (40 men).

Supply Company (7 officers, 174 men) (270 men in Panther Battalion)

Company HQ (3 officers, 19 men); Medical Detachment (1 officer, 7 men) (8 men in Panther Battalion); Maintenance Detachment (2 officers, 87 men) (164 men in Panther Battalion); Fuel Detachment (12 men) (26 men in Panther Battalion); Munitions Detachment (15 men) (18 men in Panther Battalion); Supply Detachment (1 officer, 34 men) (35 men in Panther Battalion).

Four Companies (3 officers, 100 men)

Each consisted of: Company HQ (1 officer, 17 men); Reserve Platoon (10 men); Three Platoons, (*each* 1 officer *or* NCO and 24 men).

Total strength of 752 all ranks (26 officers and 726 men), or 848 men (26 officers and 822 men) in Panther Battalion.

The Panzer Company

Reduced to three tank platoons. Each platoon had five tanks.

Notes

Notes

Notes

Notes

Notes